Winds of Worship

12 Hymn Arrangements for One or More Wind Players
Arranged by Stan Pethel

PUBLICATIONS AVAILABLE:

SB 1005 Piano / Score $12.95

SB 1006 Flute (oboe, violin) $12.95

SB 1007 B♭ Trumpet (B♭ clarinet) $12.95

SB 1008 F Horn $12.95

SB 1009 Trombone / Tuba (cello) $12.95

Shawnee Press
EXCLUSIVELY DISTRIBUTED BY

HAL•LEONARD® CORPORATION
7777 W. BLUEMOUND RD. P.O. BOX 13819 MILWAUKEE, WI 53213

PREFACE

Winds of Worship was designed to allow for maximum flexibility of use. The uses range from full ensemble to solo instrument and piano. All of the arrangements will work with or without piano, just start at the first double bar or the pickups to the first double bar.

Here are some options:

1. Solo instrument and piano or track. The piano/score book works as accompaniment for all instruments as does the accompaniment CD.

2. Multiple instruments and piano or track. Just have one instrument play the solo part and the other(s) the ensemble part along with the piano or accompaniment CD. Use more players on the solo part if needed to project the melody.

3. For instruments only, with no piano or CD accompaniment, these combinations will work:

   a. Brass Quartet – trumpet 1 & 2 with trombone 1 & 2 parts will stand alone. Start at the first double bar.

   b. Brass Quintet or Brass Sextet – For quintet use trumpet 1 & 2, horn, trombone 1, and tuba. For sextet add trombone 2. Start at the double bar.

   c. Other ensemble combinations. As long as trumpet 1 & 2 and trombone 1 & 2 are covered, the other parts will only add to the fullness of the ensemble. Piano adds even more and fills out the harmony. For instruments only start at the double bar, with piano starting at the beginning.

   d. Remember these instrumental substitutions. Violins and oboes can play or double the flute part. Clarinets can play or double the trumpet parts. Cellos, bassoons, and baritones can play the trombone part. Bass trombone players may want to try the tuba part as well. The tuba part can also be covered by a bass setting from an electric keyboard to add depth to the sound.

The difficulty level for these arrangements range from grade 2 ½ to 3. They are good lengths for preludes, offertories, and featured instrumental performance in both church services as well as church or school concerts. Most are also in good vocal range should you choose to add choral or congregational singing at appropriate places.

Best wishes with these arrangements in your area of musical ministry. Let us know at Shawnee Press if you find them useful, and what else we can do to assist with your instrumental needs.

Stan Pethel

CONTENTS

Immortal, Invisible

4

Trumpet (Clarinet, Tenor Sax, Baritone TC)
Solo

TRADITIONAL WELSH MELODY
Arranged by **STAN PETHEL**

Immortal, Invisible

Trumpet (Clarinet)
Ensemble

TRADITIONAL WELSH MELODY
Arranged by **STAN PETHEL**

Take My Life and Let It Be

Trumpet (Clarinet, Tenor Sax, Baritone TC)
Solo

Music by **HENRY A. CÉSAR MALAN**
Arranged by **STAN PETHEL**

Take My Life and Let It Be

Trumpet (Clarinet)
Ensemble

Music by **HENRY A. CÉSAR MALAN**
Arranged by **STAN PETHEL**

SOLE SELLING AGENT: SHAWNEE PRESS, INC., NASHVILLE, TN 37212

Joyful, Joyful, We Adore Thee

Trumpet (Clarinet, Tenor Sax, Baritone TC)
Solo

Music by **LUDWIG van BEETHOVEN**
Arranged by **STAN PETHEL**

Joyful, Joyful, We Adore Thee

Trumpet (Clarinet)
Ensemble

Music by **LUDWIG van BEETHOVEN**
Arranged by **STAN PETHEL**

Near to the Heart of God

Trumpet (Clarinet, Tenor Sax, Baritone TC)
Solo

Music by **CLELAND McAFEE**
Arranged by **STAN PETHEL**

Near to the Heart of God

Trumpet (Clarinet)
Ensemble

Music by **CLELAND B. McAFEE**
Arranged by **STAN PETHEL**

Praise the Lord Who Reigns Above

Trumpet (Clarinet, Tenor Sax, Baritone TC)
Solo

Foundry Collection, 1742
Arranged by **STAN PETHEL**

Praise the Lord Who Reigns Above

Trumpet (Clarinet)
Ensemble

Foundry Collection, 1742
Arranged by **STAN PETHEL**

Love Lifted Me

Trumpet (Clarinet, Tenor Sax, Baritone TC)
Solo

Music by **HOWARD E. SMITH**
Arranged by **STAN PETHEL**

Love Lifted Me

Trumpet (Clarinet)
Ensemble

Music by **HOWARD E. SMITH**
Arranged by **STAN PETHEL**

Like a River Glorious

Trumpet (Clarinet, Tenor Sax, Baritone TC)
Solo

Music by **JAMES MOUNTAIN**
Arranged by **STAN PETHEL**

Like a River Glorious

Trumpet (Clarinet)
Ensemble

Music by **JAMES MOUNTAIN**
Arranged by **STAN PETHEL**

I Will Sing of the Mercies

Trumpet (Clarinet, Tenor Sax, Baritone TC)
Solo

Music by **JAMES H. FILLMORE**
Arranged by **STAN PETHEL**

I Will Sing of the Mercies

Trumpet (Clarinet)
Ensemble

Music by **JAMES H. FILLMORE**
Arranged by **STAN PETHEL**

Savior, Like a Shepherd Lead Us

Trumpet (Clarinet, Tenor Sax, Baritone TC)
Solo

Music by **WILLIAM B. BRADBURY**
Arranged by **STAN PETHEL**

Savior, Like a Shepherd Lead Us

Trumpet (Clarinet)
Ensemble

Music by **WILLIAM B. BRADBURY**
Arranged by **STAN PETHEL**

Higher Ground

Trumpet (Clarinet, Tenor Sax, Baritone TC)
Solo

Music by **CHARLES H. GABRIEL**
Arranged by **STAN PETHEL**

Higher Ground

Trumpet (Clarinet)
Ensemble

Music by **CHARLES H. GABRIEL**
Arranged by **STAN PETHEL**

My Jesus, I Love Thee

Trumpet (Clarinet, Tenor Sax, Baritone TC)
Solo

Music by **ADONIRAM J. GORDON**
Arranged by **STAN PETHEL**

My Jesus, I Love Thee

Trumpet (Clarinet)
Ensemble

Music by **ADONIRAM J. GORDON**
Arranged by **STAN PETHEL**

He's Got the Whole World in His Hands

Trumpet (Clarinet, Tenor Sax, Baritone TC)
Solo

TRADITIONAL SPIRITUAL
Arranged by **STAN PETHEL**

He's Got the Whole World in His Hands

Trumpet (Clarinet)
Ensemble

TRADITIONAL SPIRITUAL
Arranged by **STAN PETHEL**

HYMN STORIES

He's Got the Whole World in His Hands

African-American Spirituals were first heard by the world at large in the 1870s, shortly after black Americans were emancipated due to the Civil War. A group of ex-slaves, known as The Fisk Jubilee Singers, toured the United States and Britain with renditions using orchestra.

Many listeners were amazed at the originality and energy of what they heard. Music in the western part of the world soon showed this influence. Spirituals rescued faithful black Christians from "sinkin' down." Now these unique songs added vitality to the music idioms of the world. "He's Got the Whole World in His Hands" is one of those songs.

Higher Ground

This hymn was written by a businessman, Johnson Oatman, Jr. It has been a favorite with many Christians since it was first published in 1898. It expresses so well a universal desire for a deeper spiritual life, continuing to a higher plane of fellowship with God than we have ever experienced before.

In his leisure time, Mr. Oatman wrote about 3,000 Gospel songs. Though ordained by the Methodist Episcopal denomination, he never pastored a church. Despite the fact his Hymns were well received, he was never paid more than $1.00 for each of his texts.

I Will Sing of the Mercies

This well-loved chorus has been sung now for generations. It has become a modern-day classic in the church and has found its way into some hymnals. With its up-beat feel, it is often used near the beginning of worship services. The music was written by James H. Fillmore. The words, based on Psalms 89:1, speak of God's unfailing mercy and His faithfulness throughout all generations.

Immortal, Invisible

This well-known hymn is from W. C. Smith's *Hymns of Christ and the Christian Life,* 1867. It is based upon I Timothy 1:17; 'Now unto the King eternal, immortal, invisible, the only wise God, be honor and glory for ever and ever'. The reference to 'the Ancient of Days' in the third line of verse one comes from Daniel 7:9, while the third line of verse two echoes Psalm 36:6; 'Thy righteousness is like the great mountains.' Walter Chalmers Smith (1824-1908) was born and educated in Scotland.

The powerful tune for this hymn is called 'St. Denio'. Also known as 'Joanna', it is based upon a Welsh folk-song. There are actually several possible sources, the most likely being a ballad of about 1810, *'Can Mlynedd i'nawr'* ('A hundred years from now'). Other sources suggest a ballad about a cuckoo. First printed as a hymn tune in John Robert's *Caniadau y Cyssegr,* 1839, it was then called 'Palestina'. The tune was first introduced into mainstream hymnody by Gustav Holst in *The English Hymnal,* 1906.

Joyful, Joyful, We Adore Thee

The tune for this hymn comes from Beethoven's 9th symphony, and is known as "Hymn of Joy." The words were written by Henry van Dyke, born in Pennsylvania in 1852, and who became the pastor of the Brick Presbyterian Church in New York City. He was inspired to write the hymn at the sight of the beautiful Berkshire Mountains before preaching a message at Williams College in Massachusetts.

Many have found the words to be inspiring: *"Melt the clouds of sin and sadness, drive the dark of doubt away. Giver of immortal gladness, fill us with the light of day."* This is a prayer set to song. Van Dyke later became the professor of English literature at Princeton University. He also held a number of other prominent positions, including American Ambassador to the Netherlands, and was a personal friend of President Woodrow Wilson.

Like a River Glorious

Frances Havergal, while vacationing in the south of Wales in 1876, caught a severe cold and her lungs became inflamed. She was told she might die as a result. She said that would be too good to be true. Her friends were amazed at the peace with which she faced the prospect of dying. That same year Frances wrote these words: *Like a river glorious, is God's perfect peace, Over all victorious, in its bright increase; Perfect, yet it floweth, fuller every day, Perfect, yet it groweth, deeper all the way. Stayed upon Jehohvah, hearts are fully blest Finding, as He promised, perfect peace and rest.*

Three years later, Frances ran into some cold, wet weather while telling some boys about the Lord. She grew ill and it became apparent Frances was dying. When told one day by one of her doctors she would probably die soon, she responded by saying, "Beautiful, too good to be true." Later that day, after experiencing a series of convulsions, the nurse laid her head back on the pillow.

The following account was recorded by her sister: "Then she looked up steadfastly, as if she saw the Lord. Surely nothing less heavenly could have reflected such a glorious radiance upon her face. For ten minutes we watched that almost visible meeting with her King, and her countenance was so glad, as if she were already talking to Him! Then she tried to sing, but after one sweet, high note, "HE . . . ," her voice failed and her brother commended her soul into the Redeemer's hand."

Love Lifted Me

Working together to write the hymn, one man paced as he thought out the words, the other sat at the piano as he hammered out the tune. James Rowe was the lyricist and his friend, Howard E. Smith, the pianist. Those who knew Howard wondered how he could play at all, since his hands were so disfigured by arthritis.

Born on the first day of 1865, Rowe was the English son of a copper miner, and later immigrated to the United States. Having married in Albany, New York, he got a job with the railroad. Eventually, he became a full-time writer, composing hymns and editing music journals for several publishers.

During his lifetime, Rowe claimed to have written over 19,000 song texts. "Love Lifted Me" was written by James Rowe in collaboration with Howard E. Smith in Saugatuck, Connecticut in 1912. Copyrights to the hymn were eventually transferred to Robert Coleman for the price of one hundred dollars.

My Jesus, I Love Thee

William Ralph Featherston was born in 1846 in the city of Montreal. He died in the same city at age 26. He and his family attended a Wesleyan Methodist Church. It appears likely William wrote this hymn as a poem after having accepted Christ as Lord and Savior.

He reportedly sent the poem to his Aunt in California. Somehow, it then appeared as an anonymous hymn in a British hymnal in 1864. William was only 16 years old when he wrote these words: *"My Jesus, I love Thee, I know Thou art mine. For Thee, all the follies Of sin I resign."*

Near to the Heart of God

Rev. Armstrong McAffee wrote an original hymn for his church choir each quarter at Communion. He usually wrote his stanzas to reinforce the theme for his sermons. His congregation began to anticipate their Pastor's hymns as much as the sermons themselves.

When Rev. McAffee's brother tragically lost his two daughters to diphtheria, their close-knit families offered the bereaved parents all the love, understanding and sympathy possible. On the following Sunday, the young Pastor's sermon bore this theme: "We can find peace and comfort if we stay near to the heart of God." As for the hymn, here are a few of the words that flowed from his pen: *"There is a place of quiet rest, Near to the heart of God; A place where sin cannot molest, Near to the heart of God."*

Praise the Lord Who Reigns Above

Charles Wesley, born in England in 1707, is the writer of this hymn. He is sometimes described as the "first Methodist." He and his brother, John were the first to bring together a group of like-minded Christians at Oxford University known as the "Holy Club."

During this time, Charles had an experience with the Lord. He spoke of a "strange palpitation of the heart." Three days later, John felt his own heart "strangely warmed." Charles usually deferred to the leadership of John. Charles wrote hundreds of hymns and was a very prolific poet in the English language. Today, Charles Wesley's hymns are actually better remembered than John's sermons.

Savior, Like a Shepherd Lead Us

One Christmas Eve, Ira D. Sankey was traveling by steamboat. Asked to sing, he sang the Shepherd Song. Afterward, a man came up to Mr. Sankey and asked if he had fought for the North during the Civil War. Mr. Sankey confirmed he had. The stranger had fought for the South. After further questions, the two men determined they had been in the same place, years before.

One moonlit night, while concealed in shadow, the southern soldier was about to fire a shot that certainly would have killed the northern soldier. "But the song you sang then was the song you sang just now," said the old confederate. "I heard the words perfectly: *We are Thine, do Thou befriend us, Be the guardian of our way.* "When you had finished your song, it was impossible for me to take aim at you again. I thought: 'The Lord who is able to save that man from certain death must surely be great and mighty,' and my arm of its own accord dropped limp at my side."

Take My Life and Let It Be

Take My Life and Let It Be was written in 1874 by English born Francis Havergal. She left the following account: "I went for a little visit of five days. There were ten persons in the house; some were unconverted and long prayed for, some converted but not rejoicing Christians. He gave me the prayer, 'Lord, give me all in this house.' And He just did. Before I left the house, everyone had got a blessing. The last night of my visit, I was too happy to sleep and passed most of the night in renewal of my consecration, and these little couplets formed themselves and chimed in my heart one after another 'til they finished with 'ever only, all for Thee!'"

Miss Havergal did not speak her words lightly. She later wrote to a friend: The Lord has shown me another little step, and, of course, I have taken it with extreme delight. 'Take my silver and my gold' now means shipping off all my ornaments to the church Missionary House, including a jewel cabinet that is really fit for a countess, where all will be accepted and disposed of for me... I don't think I ever packed a box with such pleasure.

Dr. Stan Pethel is a Professor of Music and Chair of Fine Arts at Berry College near Rome, Georgia. He has been on the music faculty at Berry College since 1973. He holds a Bachelor of Music, and Master of Fine Arts degrees from the University of Georgia and a Doctorate of Musical Arts degree from the University of Kentucky. In addition to his duties as Chair of Fine Arts at Berry College Dr. Pethel teaches music theory, composition and arranging, world music, and low brass lessons.

He is a widely published composer and arranger with over 1000 works in publication with 26 different publishers. His writing includes works for choir, piano, organ/piano duet, symphonic band, jazz ensemble, orchestra, hand bells, solo instrument and piano, and various chamber music ensembles.

He is married to Jo Ann Pethel, a pianist and music educator. They have three grown children: Mary Ellen, college history teacher; Rob, a missionary with the International Mission Board; and Joseph, a physical education teacher.

HAL·LEONARD® TRUMPET PLAY-ALONG

The Trumpet Play-Along Series will help you play your favorite songs quickly and easily. Just follow the printed music, listen to the sound-alike recordings and hear how the trumpet should sound, and then play along using the separate backing tracks.

1. POPULAR HITS

Copacabana (At the Copa) (Barry Manilow) • Does Anybody Really Know What Time It Is? (Chicago) • Hot Hot Hot (Buster Poindexter) • Livin' La Vida Loca (Ricky Martin) • Ring of Fire (Johnny Cash) • Sir Duke (Stevie Wonder) • Sussudio (Phil Collins) • Will It Go Round in Circles (Billy Preston).

00137383 Book/Online Audio $16.99

2. TRUMPET CLASSICS

Ciribiribin (Harry James) • Feels So Good (Chuck Mangione) • Java (Al Hirt) • Music to Watch Girls By (Bob Crewe Generation) • Spanish Flea (Herb Alpert) • Sugar Blues (Al Hirt) • A Taste of Honey (Herb Alpert) • The Toy Trumpet (Raymond Scott).

00137384 Book/Online Audio $16.99

3. CLASSIC ROCK

All You Need Is Love (The Beatles) • Deacon Blues (Steely Dan) • Feelin' Stronger Every Day (Chicago) • Higher Love (Steve Winwood) • September (Earth, Wind & Fire) • Spinning Wheel (Blood, Sweat & Tears) • 25 or 6 to 4 (Chicago) • Vehicle (Ides of March).

00137385 Book/Online Audio $16.99

4. GREAT THEMES

Cherry Pink and Apple Blossom White (Perez Prado) • Deborah's Theme (Ennio Morricone) • Dragnet (Walter Schumann) • The Godfather Waltz (Nino Rota) • Gonna Fly Now (Bill Conti) • Green Hornet Theme (Al Hirt) • The Odd Couple (Neal Hefti) • Sugar Lips (Al Hirt).

00137386 Book/Online Audio $16.99

6. MILES DAVIS

Airegin • Bye Bye Blackbird • Doxy • E.S.P. • Half Nelson • Move • So What • Summertime.

00137447 Book/Online Audio $16.99

7. JAZZ BALLADS

Body and Soul • Easy Living • Everything Happens to Me • I Remember Clifford • Over the Rainbow • Stella by Starlight • They Can't Take That Away from Me • Where or When.

00137475 Book/Online Audio $16.99

HAL·LEONARD®

www.halleonard.com

Prices, contents, and availability subject to change without notice.